FORERUNNERS: IDEAS FIRST FROM THE UNIVERSITY OF
MINNESOTA PRESS

Original e-works to spark new scho'

FORERUNNERS: IDEAS FIRST is ~ocess series of
breakthrough digital works. v ideas and fin-
ished books, Forerunners ´ ted in nota-
ble blogs, social med¹ articles, and
the synergy of a⸍ ⸍erature publishing: where inte⸍ ⸍culation take place in
scholarship.

Clare Birchall
**Shareveillance: The Da ⸍ of Openly Sharing and Covertly
Collecting Data**

Ian Bogost
The Geek's Chihuahua: Living with Apple

William E. Connolly
**Aspirational Fascism: The Struggle for Multifaceted Democracy
under Trumpism**

Andrew Culp
Dark Deleuze

Sohail Daulatzai
Fifty Years of "The Battle of Algiers": Past as Prologue

Grant Farred
Martin Heidegger Saved My Life

David Golumbia
The Politics of Bitcoin: Software as Right-Wing Extremism

Gary Hall
The Uberfication of the University

John Hartigan Jr.
Aesop's Anthropology: A Multispecies Approach

Mark Jarzombek
Digital Stockholm Syndrome in the Post-Ontological Age

The Neocolonialism of the
Global Village

The Neocolonialism of the Global Village

Ginger Nolan

University of Minnesota Press

MINNEAPOLIS

Portions of *The Neocolonialism of the Global Village* were previously published as "Quasi-Urban Citizenship: The Global Village as '*Nomos* of the Modern,'" in *The Journal of Architecture* 23, no. 4 (May 2018), available online at http://www.tandfonline.com/.

Published by the University of Minnesota Press, 2018
111 Third Avenue South, Suite 290
Minneapolis, MN 55401–2520
http://www.upress.umn.edu

The University of Minnesota is an equal-opportunity educator and employer.

The twentieth-century encounter between alphabetic and electronic faces of culture confers on the printed word a crucial role in staying the return to Africa.

—MARSHALL McLUHAN, *Gutenberg Galaxy: The Making of Typographic Man*

Contents

1. The Global Village

THE TERM "global village" first appeared in 1962 with the publication of Marshall McLuhan's *The Gutenberg Galaxy: The Making of Typographic Man*.[1] In popular usage, the expression has assumed a utopian connotation, suggesting a perpetual peace enabled by electronic communications. In the global village, diverse cultural tradition will supposedly survive—indeed, thrive—amid the transformations wrought by electronic connectivity. But McLuhan was hardly a utopian thinker, and the magic conjured by the "global village" should be treated with some skepticism. This magic, which continues to pervade techno-humanitarian discourses, was born of colonial thought, having been coined by McLuhan in reference to various devices of British colonial and neocolonial power. What the "global village" suggests is a state of political dispossession resulting from a differential in semiotic power. The global village is constituted first and foremost by a rural subaltern that—owing to its geographic dispersion—is governed largely through nootechnologies. These latter can elide geographic distances and thereby facilitate governance over a vastly dispersed popula-

1. Marshall McLuhan, *Gutenberg Galaxy: The Making of Typographic Man* (Toronto: University of Toronto Press, 1962), 21; 31.

tion. To some extent, we are all global villagers, but given the imbalances of semiotic power (accruing to urbanites versus ruralites, to global North versus global South, and to the literate versus nonliterate), some belong more thoroughly to the global village than others.

It has gone strangely unnoted in the abundant scholarship on McLuhan that the global village seems to have been inspired by techniques of colonial rule in Africa, specifically from Britain's brutal villagization scheme in Kenya in the 1950s, in which thousands of Kikuyu, Embu, and Meru civilians from Kenya's Rift Valley were detained in camps.[2] Yet McLuhan, while copiously citing colonial research on Kenya's villagization, was clearly not depicting a future of wartime detainment camps so much as depoliticization and pacification through other means: through other media. It was not barbed-wire enclosures that would circumscribe the global community McLuhan imagined but rather feedback loops of information that were to work in tandem with spatial tactics of quasi-urbanization. The global village was modeled on colonial strategies intended to transform the semiotic, economic, and spatial fabric of the decolonizing world in such a way as to safeguard British economic and political interests in the aftermath of indepen-

2. One recent edited volume themed on McLuhan's "global village" makes no mention of McLuhan's obsession with the dangerous effects of "de-tribalization" in the colonial and postcolonial world. The one contributor who mentions McLuhan's deep intellectual debt to John Colin Carothers fails to note that Carothers's theories were based on his advisory role to Kenya's villagization. Indeed, the editors gloss the book's "transatlantic perspectives" to mean Canadian-European perspectives, neglecting the vital role that African colonialism played in McLuhan's thought. See Carmen Birkle, Angela Krewani, and Martin Kuester, eds. *McLuhan's Global Village Today: Transatlantic Perspectives* (London: Pickering & Chatto, 2014).

dence. Following the example of British strategy in Kenya, the global village can be understood as a mechanism for pacifying postcolonial agrarian society by absorbing people made landless by the relentless expansion of agrarian capital. The global village—like villagization—was intended to enfold dispossessed denizens into the incipient nation-form and into the global market, while simultaneously withholding the modes of semiotic power required to participate effectively in a public sphere.

2. Neocolonialism and Nootechnologies

THAT KENYA'S WAR should have been so influential to McLuhan's theories of media stems largely from the significance of communications technologies and semiotic rights leading up to the war and determining its outcome. In its beginnings, the Kikuyu anticolonial struggle was a campaign for rights not only to land—as is generally claimed—but also to literacy.[1] In the 1930s, the Kikuyu Central Association (KCA) launched an education campaign largely focused on English language instruction, believing that Kikuyu grievances could be redressed only by appealing to the British in their own terms, through their discourses, laws, and modes of inscription.[2] Colonial settlers forcibly shut down most of these schools, inciting the KCA to embark on a letter-writing campaign to British Parliament. Although the metropole ulti-

1. On the Kikuyu literacy campaign, see Derek Peterson, "Writing the Revolution: Independent Schooling and Mau Mau in Nyeri," in *Mau Mau and Nationhood,* ed. E. S. Atieno Odhiambo and John Lonsdale (Nairobi: EAEP; Athens: Ohio University Press; Oxford: James Currey), 76–120.
2. Peterson, "Writing the Revolution."

mately affirmed the KCA's right to formal education, settlers continued to wage violence against the Kikuyu schools after they were reopened.[3] Finally, in the early 1950s, factions of the KCA branched off into the Kenya Land and Freedom Army (KLFA), leading to the outbreak of what the British called the "Mau Mau" war.

British strategies of late-colonial warfare in Kenya construed electronic media as devices for extending soft power across different languages and levels of literacy. As the British had just learned in their war against the Malayan Communist Party in the 1940s and '50s, winning the war in Kenya would require effective means of disseminating propaganda among dispersed, linguistically diverse, and often nonliterate populations.[4] Much of the scholarship McLuhan cites in *Gutenberg Galaxy* and its sequel, *Understanding Media: The Extensions of Man*, revolved around late-colonial concerns over whether Africans should be allowed to acquire literacy and of the impact film and radio had on Africans' thoughts and habits. In Kenya, newspapers and pamphlets provided a cheap and fairly effective way of disseminating colonial propaganda, given relatively high rates of literacy. However, the colonial administration perceived that literacy could easily become a device of anticolonial politics, as attested, for example, by Tom Mboya's newspaper *Uhuru*, which the British sought to proscribe following the outbreak of war.[5]

3. Peterson, "Writing the Revolution."

4. On the use of Psy-Ops in Kenya, see "Notes from Psychological Warfare Staff, 1956" in TNA FCO141/6473. Meeting minutes describe the need for broadcast media in the forests of Kenya's Rift Valley as a form of wartime propaganda.

5. "One of Mboya's instruments is the African newspaper which he owns called 'Uhuru' . . . [which] was very largely instrumental in encouraging the growth of the Kenyatta cult [i.e., the anticolonial resis-

The problem of colonial communications was both semiotic and spatial: While literacy was to be discouraged for
its dangerous political effects, access to radio receivers was
hardly feasible for agriculturalists dispersed throughout the
countryside. In answer to this dilemma, villagization—already
underway as a method of attrition—provided a ready expedi-
ent. By agglomerating Kenyans in these compact camps, detainees could be easily reached by traveling radio and cinema
vans, circumventing urban density and literacy as means of
facilitating the spread of propaganda.[6] Insofar as villagization appears to have been a model for McLuhan (a point I will
come to presently), the global village should be understood as
a quasi-urban device for militating against the semiotic—and
thus political—power of agrarian societies in the colonized
and formerly colonized world.

To excavate this genealogy of the global village is to stress
the neocolonial and class-based dimensions of noopolitics,
pointing to how nootechnologies (technologies of the mind)
have operated through the global division of labor they help
produce, through media differentials bound up with construc-
tions of race and with divisions between the rural and urban.
This essay therefore pushes dominant critiques of noopolitics,
such as Bernard Stielger's, into the domain of postcolonial
critique, identifying a fraught site where noopolitics helped
bind together a dense conflux of power.[7] Because various arch-

---

tance led by Jomo Kenyatta]. Another instrument at Mboya's disposal is
the very large number of unemployed Africans ... who have drifted into
Nairobi from the reserves." TNA CAB/129/96, 1.

6. Brian Larkin gives some history of the use of traveling cinema
vans by the British in Nigeria as means of indirect rule. See Larkin,
Signal and Noise: Media, Infrastructure, and Urban Culture in Nigeria
(Durham, N.C.: Duke University Press, 2008), chapters 1 and 3.

7. I refer to a number of Stiegler's works here, including the

paradigms of power—biopolitics, noopolitics, capital, colonialism, and what I will call "terra-power"—all were implicated in villagization, I will not focus exclusively on any one of these but rather on their interaction as they converged and crystallized into the notion of the global village.

It is often claimed that the advent of electronic communications has caused a dematerialization of many things—of place, of representation, of sociality, and of economic exchange, to name a few. While there is no lack of scholars who, to the contrary, insist on the materiality of media and on its imbrication with other material relations, it is the purpose of this essay to push in a slightly different direction from that body of work, by showing how the power of electronic media was and continues to be enmeshed in a reorganization of a very substratal basis of materiality: a reorganization of land, of its cultivation, settlement, and ownership. Against assumptions that electronic media have been developed first and foremost as instruments of professionalized intellectual labor, late-twentieth-century researchers and scholars of communication technologies frequently pointed toward Third World agriculturalists as ideal subjects for these technologies, a tendency that continues up through the present.[8] Electronic media have been touted as devices for integrating agrarian

---

Symbolic Misery (La Misére Symbolique) series and *Taking Care of Youth and the Generations* (*Prendre Soin, De la jeunesse et des générations*), trans. Stephen Barker (Stanford, Calif.: Stanford University Press, 2010).

8. On the early conceptualization of a relation between computer technologies, agriculture, and the peasantry, refer to discussions in the journal *AGORA* in the 1970s and 1980s. Also see "Media Arts" in Ginger Nolan, *Savage Mind to Savage Machine: Techniques and Disciplines of Creativity, c. 1880–1985* (Doctoral dissertation, Columbia University, 2015).

people into the global market (and making them directly bear the risks of that market's vicissitudes), in lieu of other communicative media such as print, which had in other parts of the world helped enfold agricultural classes into the cultural and political fabric of nation and empire.

3. "Re-tribalization"

IN 1954, shortly following the outbreak of war in Kenya's Rift Valley, the ethnopsychiatrist John Colin Carothers was called to Nairobi to diagnose the uprising and recommend strategies for pacifying Kenyans amidst the social and economic upheavals caused by the expansion of cash-crop production.[1] In an article abundantly cited by McLuhan, "Culture, Society, and the Written Word," Carothers argued that "the African mind" was shaped by orality and by its arboreal environment, and that literacy and urban life would radically upset its fragile psychological constitution.[2] Owing to these dangers, he had recommended in his earlier work, *Psychology of Mau Mau*, that villagization remain intact following the conclusion of war, not for purposes of military detainment but rather as "the whole

1. For a summary of Carothers's activities in Kenya, see Jock McCulloch, *Colonial Psychiatry and the African Mind* (Cambridge: Cambridge University Press, 1995), chapter 5.
2. Carothers summarizes his theory on the relation between nonliteracy and magical thought in the article McLuhan cites: "Culture, Society, and the Written Word," *Psychiatry*, November 1959. However, Carothers first explained these ideas, at much greater length in a book written shortly after having been sent to Kenya: *The African Mind in Health and Disease* (Geneva: World Health Organization, 1953).

future of Kikuyu rural life."[3] The Kikuyu, owing to their innate "forest psychology," would benefit, he reasoned, from "forest villages," which, though still arboreal, would provide a stabilizing social fabric.[4]

Carothers's depiction of the Kikuyu as isolated and arboreal was hardly accurate. Even apart from the Kikuyu's structures of social and political organization, there was a tendency during the first half of the twentieth century toward urbanization. Having been largely relegated to overcrowded native reserves and thus lacking adequate land for cultivation, many Kikuyu men had relocated to the outskirts of Mombasa and especially Nairobi. The colonial administration believed that Nairobi's resulting density and high unemployment rates had greatly contributed to the state of political unrest.[5] Kikuyu urbanization was therefore considered as dangerous as Kikuyu literacy. Carothers's preoccupation with the putative arboreal nature of the Kikuyu (and of Africans in general) was clearly prompted by a colonial imperative to justify the de-urbanization of black Africans by furnishing a cognitive-semiotic rationale for making villagization a permanent fixture of Kikuyu society, even following the conclusion of war.

Subscribing to prevailing colonial notions of the deleterious effects of "detribalization" on Africans, Carothers adduced a psychiatric-environmental cause for Africans' allegedly nonurban and nonliterate habitus. His central thesis on "the African

3. J. C. Carothers, *Psychology of Mau Mau* (Nairobi: Government Press, 1955), 22–23.

4. Carothers, *Psychology of Mau Mau*, 22–23.

5. "Kenya Plan for the Rehabilitation and Reabsorption of Mau Mau Detainees, Convicts, and Displaced Persons," September 27, 1955, TNA FCO 141/6263. See also TNA CAB/129/96, 1. See also Evelyn Baring to W.A.C. Mathieson, Colonial Office, London; September 8, 1956, TNA FCO 141/6263.

mind" described how the primordial darkness of Africa's forests had long occluded visual knowledge of the world, en-
shrouding Africans in an auditory sensorium that provoked
oral rather than written forms of communication.[6] He con-
trasted the psychological effects of this aural semiosis to those
of reading and writing. The physical distance between reader
and author dissipated the latter's authority, dispelling the en-
chanting power exercised by the spoken word.[7] (It should be
noted that Jomo Kenyatta, the KCA's imprisoned leader, was
considered a prodigiously gifted orator.) In liberating readers
from unthinking obedience to the magical authority of voice,
the written word conferred on them the detached intellectual
objectivity required of self-ruling subjects. Carothers conclud-
ed that illiterate society remained incapable of self-rule, being
inherently beholden to authoritarian magic. He was not, however, advocating universal education as a basis of postcolonial
independence, since particular environmental conditions, such
as the darkness of Africa's forests, irrevocably disposed societies to either orality or literacy.[8]

Carothers's claims were clearly seminal to McLuhan's renowned thesis on different media's formative effects on cognitive and cultural disposition and on his related concept of media environments. (A discussion of Carothers's ideas of literate
versus nonliterate cognition consumes roughly the first twenty
pages of *Gutenberg Galaxy,* and appears immediately under his
section heading "The new electronic interdependence rec-

6. Carothers, *The African Mind,* 36 and 180–81.

7. Carothers, *The African Mind,* 110–11 and 120–24

8. Carothers, *The African Mind,* 36 and 180–81. Carothers later fell
into step with colonial administrators' insistence that postwar rehabilitation involve programs of education, including Christian education,
largely as means of political pacification. See Carothers, *Psychology of
Mau Mau,* 25–27.

reates the world in the image of a global village."[9] Carothers is cited again in the first pages of *Understanding Media*.) McLuhan's attraction to Carothers's work seems prompted not only by the latter's keen interest in the differences between written and aural semiotics but in the political implications of connecting semiotics to race. The overlap between Carothers's and McLuhan's concerns can be seen especially in their shared qualms about African "detribalization," a term McLuhan employs exhaustively in *Gutenberg Galaxy* and *Understanding Media*.[10]

Several years prior to publishing those books, McLuhan had been very active in an interdisciplinary group, Explorations, which he cofounded with Jacqueline Tyrwhitt, a British urban planner whose work focused on village planning in the decolonizing world.[11] This connection has been investigated by the architectural historian Olga Touloumi, who argues that the idea of the global village likely was influenced by a modernist exhibition on village planning attended by Tyrwhitt and McLuhan.[12] In 1954, Tyrwhitt wrote to McLuhan of her preoccupation with the processes of detribalization caused by "a self-contained rural tradition being invaded by technology."[13] To preserve ru-

9. McLuhan, *Gutenberg Galaxy*, 31.

10. Additionally, in *Gutenberg Galaxy* and *Understanding Media*, various conjugations of "tribal" appear 101 times, and "primitive" 51 times.

11. On Tyrwhitt and self-help planning, see Ijlal Muzaffar, "Modern Architecture and the Making of the Third World" (PhD thesis, Massachusetts Institute of Technology, 2007).

12. Olga Touloumi has not yet published this material, so I am citing our personal conversations.

13. Tyrwhitt to McLuhan, May 16, 1954, as cited in Michael Darroch, "Giedion and Explorations: Confluences of Space and Media in Toronto School Theorization," in *Media Transatlantic: Developments in Media and Communication Studies between North American and*

ral culture against such transformations, Tyrwhitt advocated self-help architectures—housing built personally by occupants within certain prescriptive frameworks formulated by international experts. As Ijlal Muzaffar has argued, this self-help architectural movement of the mid-twentieth century worked to instate an intentionally incomplete and impoverished version of "modernity" in the global South amidst decolonization.[14] Planners justified this cost-saving tactic by citing the need to preserve cultural tradition against the detribalizing effects of architectural and economic modernization. For these reasons, *inter alia,* self-help architecture was considered a crucial and rehabilitative component of Kenya's villagization.[15]

The semiotic counterpart to an architecture that buffered Kenyans from detribalization was a mode of communication guarding them from the dangers of literacy while also appealing

---

German-Speaking Europe, ed. Norm Friesen (Switzerland: Springer International Publishing, 2016), 159. See also Michael Darroch and Janine Marchessault, "Anonymous History as Methodology: The Collaborations of Sigfried Giedion, Jaqueline Tyrwhitt, and the *Explorations* Group (1951–55)," in *Place Studies in Art, Media, Science, and Technology: Historical Investigations on the Sites and the Migration of Knowledge,* ed., Andreas Broeckmann and Gunalan Nadarajan (Weimar: VDG, 2008), 9–27.

14. Muzaffar, "Modern Architecture and the Making of the Third World."

15. In 1953, responding to the outbreak of war in Kenya, the secretary of state for the Colonies sent Kenya's administrators a report prepared by G. A. Atkinson, the colonial liaison officer in Building Research who cited the self-help architecture of military villagization in Malaya as the most impressive of colonial housing schemes in Asia. See TNA, CO 822/481. Subsequently, a letter from the colonial treasury notes that self-help housing in the detainment camps would be necessary from an economic standpoint but also because "the value of the detainees undertaking the work themselves is of the greatest importance from the rehabilitation standpoint." See letter from Treasury on March 31, 1954, TNA FCO 141/5688.

to their supposed semiotic dispositions. A former Cambridge classmate of McLuhan (mentioned briefly in his notebooks) argued that winning Britain's war against the KLFA was largely about leveraging *native* forms of media.[16] A propos of Kenya's war, he wrote that, in Africa,

> the main way in which ideas and impressions and news was spread from tribe to tribe and within a tribe was through the medium of the dance and song. It may be that certain Africans would prefer to get their ideas in a normal European way, but there are an immense number who would get those ideas more quickly and clearly if they were conveyed in what I would call *the African medium*. I am not in a position, and my colleagues were not in a position, to say what these African media are, but I think they should be studied and . . . we must approach the whole problem of African progression not simply with the eyes and viewpoint of Europeans, but taking into consideration the sort of things which appeal traditionally to the African mind [emphasis added].[17]

McLuhan subsequently likened the effects of radio (the most important vehicle of late-colonial propaganda) to "tribal drums."[18] It can be readily inferred from *Gutenberg Galaxy* and *Understanding Media* that the global-ness of the global village was premised not on equitable universal access to electronic media but on a certain kinship McLuhan drew between the sensoria produced respectively by oral and electronic means of communication.[19] Contrasting the enveloping rhythms of

16. McLuhan describes Alport in his notes on Cambridge Union Society debates. See Graham Larkin, "Finally Getting the Message: McLuhan's Media Practice." Lecture delivered at the Canadian Embassy, Berlin, in 2011. Transcript available at https://mcluhan.consortium.io/.

17. C. J. M. Alport, "Kenya's Answer to the Mau Mau Challenge," *African Affairs* 53, no. 212 (July 1954): 241–48.

18. McLuhan, *Understanding Media,* chapter 30: "Radio: The Tribal Drum."

19. See "Radio: The Tribal Drum," in *Understanding Media,* 297–307.

"tribal drums" and radio to the rational, detached experience of reading print (an experience he considered as intellectually liberating as it was sensually stultifying), McLuhan suggested that thanks to the advent of electronic media, "Western man" could now experience both the intellectual autonomy won through centuries of typographic culture and the more direct sensory experience of aurality as practiced by "tribal" societies.[20] However, the "tribal" world—a term that enfolded conceptions of race, semiotic disposition, and agrarianism— was to become subject to electronic media without having first passed through the crucible of typographic culture. McLuhan explained that although "we" now can understand "the native or non-literate experience because we have re-created it electronically within our own culture," nonetheless, *post-literacy is a quite different mode . . . from pre-literacy.*"[21] The distinction was an important one.

Whereas nonliterate societies, according to McLuhan, dwell unconsciously in the habitus produced by aurality, the post-typographic people of the Western world could—thanks to electronic media—freely, *consciously* move between the two cognitive paradigms of the aural and typographic, effectively experiencing the sensual richness of the "tribal" while keeping one foot firmly planted in the apperceptive episteme born of typography. "For the electric," writes McLuhan, "puts the mythic or collective dimension of human experience fully into the conscious wake-a-day world . . . While the old . . . cycles had been

---

20. For example, McLuhan writes: "The subliminal depths of radio are charged with the resonating echoes of tribal horns and antique drums. This is inherent in the very nature of the medium, with its power to turn the psyche and society into a single echo chamber." *Understanding Media,* 299.

21. McLuhan, *Gutenberg Galaxy,* 46, emphasis added.

tribally entranced in the collective night of the unconscious, the new . . . cycle of totally interdependent man must be lived in the light of consciousness."[22]

Absolutely undermining his hallmark thesis that a society's dominant medium determines its cultural and political disposition, McLuhan indicates that the cultural effects of electronic audio and audiovisual media would be vastly different in "tribal" versus "post-typographic" societies. We deduce from his arguments that it is *not* in fact media that shapes cultural-political subjectivity so much as a society's *previous* modes of media reception, modes apparently transmitted epigenetically over the course of centuries and across generations, mysteriously persisting even as new forms of media replace the old ones. So long as the psyche of "Western man" had *once* been formed by typography, a cognitive and cultural difference would continue to distinguish "the West" from societies that had supposedly overleapt print media in their shift from the "tribal drum" to its electronic version, radio. Betraying his seminal claim that "the medium is the message," McLuhan suggests that "the message" is really preencoded in the racial constitution of the audience or reader.

It seems contextually significant that at the time McLuhan was writing these two major works on media theory, North American civil rights movements were calling attention to discriminatory policies of administering literacy tests to black would-be voters in the United States and Canada. That is, while McLuhan insisted that the cognitive *inheritance* of typography protected "Western man" from the intellectually infantilizing effects of the West's new nonliterate media, the "grandfather clause" in the southern United States exempted white voters

22. McLuhan, *Gutenberg Galaxy,* 269.

from the literacy requirements imposed on black voters, implying that literacy—and the political rights based on literacy—were to be acquired not through personal education so much as through racial inheritance. In McLuhan's work, the hegemonic potentials of electronic media were supported by the belief that "Western man" would retain some inherited cognitive resistance against the "tribalizing" effects of electronic media; that the culture instated by the printed word would outlive print's obsolescence amidst electronic media. The West's typographic legacy played, according to McLuhan, "a crucial role in staying the return to Africa."[23]

23. McLuhan, *Gutenberg Galaxy*, 45.

4. From Global Market to Global Village

AS EARLY AS THE 1940s, several colonial agricultural experts had urged Kenya's local administration to remove the regulatory mechanisms preventing black Kenyans from cultivating tea and coffee.[1] The outbreak of war in 1952 combined with Roger Swynnerton's promotion in 1954 to the position of deputy director of agriculture in Kenya gave the necessary impetus to finally impose reforms leading to the creation of a class of black, cash-crop plantation owners. This class, in aligning its political and economic interests with white plantation owners, was intended to guarantee the security of the existing cash-crop system.[2] Collaboration between a black and white bourgeoisie would help safeguard colonial settlers' land holdings and their subsequent access to a large pool of landless, underpaid agricultural laborers.

1. For a longer discussion of Kenya's colonial agricultural policies, see Nolan, "Cash-Crop Design: Architectures of Land, Knowledge, and Alienation in Twentieth-Century Kenya," Architectural Theory and Review, No. 3 (December 2017): 280-301.

2. Roger Swynnerton, *A Plan to Intensify the Development of African Agriculture in Kenya* (Nairobi: Government Printer, 1955): 10.

Within this expanding cash-crop economy, landowners required timely information about fluctuating crop prices on the global market, underscoring the close relationship between a "free market" and "free speech," the latter including the untrammeled flow of economic information. A long-standing Anglo-American conflation of the market and the public sphere—of free trade and free speech—presented a dilemma, however, in the context of colonial martial law, villagization, and efforts to push Kenya more fully toward agrarian capitalism. The problem involved a question of media, as attested by McLuhan's notion of "market society." He claimed that the existence of "market society . . . required centuries of transformation by Gutenberg technology" and "presupposes a long period of psychic transformation" through literacy.[3] The Soviet-bloc nations failed, he said, to develop into a market society because their psychic apparatuses had not been adequately conditioned by typography.[4] If market society could only be inaugurated by a polity already liberated by the psycho-semiotic effects of print media, then the vast part of the world McLuhan described as subliterate (basically everywhere except North America and Western Europe) apparently would not belong to "market society" despite its increasing absorption in the global market. In the context of capitalist ideology, it is not difficult to see how McLuhan might attribute to market society the same cultural lineaments he ascribed to Gutenberg technologies, namely those of independent self-regulation. Since the global market was construed as self-regulating according to economic "nature," implicitly market society would be constituted by intellectually self-regulating subjects; that is, subjects

3. McLuhan, *Gutenberg Galaxy*, 272.
4. McLuhan, *Gutenberg Galaxy*, 272.

who, thanks to print technology, had been liberated from the enchantment of oral authority.

In Kenya the need for selective media connectivity—for connecting farmers to a global market without facilitating the free circulation of political expression—found expression in a particular architectural feature of villagization.

In a plan for "permanent villages" (i.e., those intended to remain even after demilitarization), Kenya's chief health inspector, Harvey Waddicar, distributed 280 single-room houses around a large central area labeled as "market open space" surrounded by a ring of "shop plots."[5] As the war had curtailed normal economic activity, Waddicar's generous allotment of market space is striking. Colonial administrators frequently bemoaned the lack of land suitable for villagization (the war having been precipitated largely by land shortages).[6] And villagization had seriously disrupted agricultural production by conscripting detainees to work on infrastructural projects in lieu of cultivating food crops. Given reports of rampant malnutrition in the detainment camps, it seems there would have been little to buy or sell in the market Waddicar delineated.[7]

5. Robert F. Gray to Walter S. Rogers, "Kikuyu Villagization," Nairobi, January 11, 1955, 2–3, in Robert F. Gray *Newsletters, 1954-56* (Institute of Current World Affairs).

6. "Kenya Plan for the Rehabilitation and Reabsorption of Mau Mau Detainees, Convicts, and Displaced Persons," September 27, 1955, from Secretary, Cabinet Office, TNA FCO 141/6263.

7. On malnutrition in the detainment camps, see the following: Marshall S. Clough, *Mau Mau Memoirs: History, Memory, and Politics* (London; Boulder, Colo.: Lynn Rienner Publishers, 1998): 157; David P. Sandgren, *Mau Mau's Children: The Making of Kenya's Postcolonial Elite* (Madison: University of Wisconsin Press, 2012), 28; and Caroline Macy Elkins, *Detention and Rehabilitation during the Mau Mau Emergencey: The Crisis of Late Colonial Kenya* (Cambridge, Mass.: Harvard University Press, 2001), 448–49.

Figure 1. Van with radio broadcast and British news services in the "new village" of Kianjogu. The National Archives, TNA CO 1066 963/22.

The allocation of such a large market space appears overdetermined by two strains of colonial strategy: first, to mark the permanent villages as a microcosms of a future agrarian capitalist society (recalling that the direct inspiration for Kenya's villagization came from Britain's recent war against the Malayan Communist Party); and second, to reiterate—in colonial form—Britain's conflation of a free market with a public sphere, albeit in this case, a public sphere violently evacuated of meaningful content. Photographs of Kenya's detainment camps show how these central areas functioned as sites of media reception for colonial psychological operations ("Psy-Ops").[8] Vans outfitted with radio broadcasting speakers parked there, disseminating

8. See photographs in TNA CO 1066.

various forms of propaganda to the gathering crowds of detainees. To designate this central space a *market* (one devoid of actual commerce but suffused with broadcast media) indicates the subjugation a two paradigms of exchange (commerce and discourse) with two paradigms of consumption (welfare rations and broadcast media).

McLuhan, who had explored the workings of advertising media in his first major book, *The Mechanical Bride,* was interested in how media governed not through their explicit content but through the cognitive environments they produced. In *Gutenberg Galaxy,* following his protracted citation of Carothers's theories, McLuhan turned to research on Britain's Colonial Film Unit in Africa to understand the effects of film on African psychology.[9] One finding of the Colonial Film Unit was, unsurprisingly, that educational films were less compelling to audiences than films intended purely as entertainment, suggesting that the latter might therefore serve as a better instrument of soft power.[10] Another observation made by researchers at the Colonial Film Unit—anticipating McLuhan's theories—was that ultimately "the content" of the medium was far less important than the cognitive habits and preferences the audience brought to bear upon their reception of the film in question.[11]

In the Colonial Film Unit's discussions, as well as in McLuhan's work, a specific idea of nootechnologies emerged, one that lo-

9. McLuhan cites at length an interview with John Wilson concerning the work of the Colonial Film Unit in Africa. McLuhan, *Gutenberg Galaxy,* 36–39.
10. "Memorandum on the results of a research into the Audience Reactions to the film, carried out in Udi Division in Feb. 1948," October 1948, TNA CO 927/83/2.
11. See "Memorandum on the results of a research into the Audience Reactions to the film" and "Report from meeting on Cinema Audience Research in Africa," October 8, 1948, TNA CO 927/83/2.

cated the power of those technologies not in the explicit content they purveyed so much as in the magical sway they held over audiences. Media did not alter minds only by implanting didactic instruction and Anglophilic imagery (the typical content of British colonial films); it altered them simply by what it *was*. As such, the "market open space" in Waddicar's plan seems to have offered a resolution to the colony's vexed predicament of how to instate a free market while discouraging the political agitation associated with free speech. The resolution is the transformation of the public sphere from a site of discourse into a site of media reception.

5. Feedback Loops/Barbed-Wire Fences

FOR MCLUHAN, a key feature of audiovisual media such as television was the "participation" or "involvement" they supposedly demanded of viewers.[1] The fact that the global village has been so frequently cast in a utopian light, interpreted by media enthusiasts as a burgeoning global democracy, surely owes something to the equivocations of terms such as "participation," which are often associated with forms of democratic discourse. Majid Rahnema has shown how the term has operated in global developmental discourses where often no distinction is made between transitive and intransitive forms of participation, the latter category including

---

1. Participation was also deemed the basis of the global village, in this case referring to the interaction of geographically disparate societies. McLuhan writes: "As electrically contracted, the globe is no more than a village. . . . It is this implosive factor that alters the position of the Negro, the teen-ager, and some other groups. They can no longer be *contained,* in the political sense of limited association. . . . This is the Age of Anxiety for the reason of the electric implosion that compels commitment and participation, quite regardless of any 'point of view.'" McLuhan, *Understanding Media,* 5.

"teleguided" and "manipulated" modes of participation.[2] True to Rahnema's analysis, in McLuhan's usage participation through audiovisual media comes as a form of pastoral power, a form of cognitive involvement underlying the notion of the global village.

The psychological nature of participation appears in McLuhan's description of social clubs, which he saw as an antecedent for participatory media, insofar as clubs and media both entailed forms of political censorship. "British clubmen," he writes, "for the sake of companionship and amiability, have long excluded the hot topics of religion and politics from mention inside the highly participational club."[3] Speculating then on the effects of "participatory" media in Africa, McLuhan displaces the British clubmen's mechanism of internal *self*-regulation with governance by electronic media:

> "We can program twenty more hours of TV in South Africa next week to cool down the tribal temperature raised by radio last week." Whole cultures could now [with television] be programmed to keep their emotional climate stable in the same way that we have begun to know something about maintaining equilibrium in the commercial economies of the world.[4]

In other words, to participate is to give oneself over to prevailing *programs,* whether dictated by club etiquette or by apartheid-based mass media. For McLuhan, the "we" who "have begun to know something" about global economic governance are also the same "we" who "can program . . . TV." Economic knowledge and media programming are linked by an epistemic disposition that allows the self-regulating sub-

2. Majid Rahnema, "Participation," in *The Development Dictionary,* ed. Wolfgang Sachs (New York: Zed Books, 2007), 116–31.

3. McLuhan, *Understanding Media,* 28

4. McLuhan, *Understanding Media,* 28.

jects of typographic culture to create self-regulating systems through which to govern. Programming provides a code according to which things can autonomously operate, can run their course without direct interference. As we will see in the case of British colonial rule, villagers' participation in a feedback loop of information was established as a precondition for the transition from barbed-wire fences to postcolonial independence, in which the nation would be allowed to run its course.

Techniques of communicative participation, first developed during Britain's war against the Malayan Communist Party, served as the key precedent for techniques later adapted to Kenya. It was in Malaya in the late 1940s that General Harold Briggs conceived the plan for villagization now referred to as Briggs' Plan, which would become a model for Kenya. The "new villages" (*kampung baru's*) were originally constructed to contain ethnic Chinese civilians so as to curtail the leakage of food and information to Communist militias. In tandem with villagization, vans and airplanes equipped with audio speakers extended a Hearts-and-Minds campaign into arboreal areas, attempting to surmount the communicative limitations imposed by rural dispersion and widespread nonliteracy.[5]

At first glance, Psy-Ops appear to have consisted of little more than crude technological improvisations, such as out-

---

5. On Psy-Ops in British Malaya, see Susan Carruthers, *Winning Hearts and Minds: British Governments, the Media, and Colonial Counter-Insurgency, 1944–1960* (Leicster, UK: Leicster University Press, 1995). See also Mohammed Azzam Mohd. Hanif Ghows, *The Malayan Emergency Revisited, 1948–1960: A Pictorial History* (Kuala Lumpur: AMR Holding; Petaling Jaya: Yayasan Pelajaran Islam, 2006) and John Coates, *Suppressing Insurgency: An Analysis of the Malayan Emergency, 1948–1954* (Boulder, Colo.: Westview Press, 1992).

fitting automobiles and airplanes with radio-broadcast technologies and, later, with film projectors.[6] However, the honing of propaganda techniques by the British and Americans during the Cold War involved epistemic as well as technological innovations, namely a convergence of three noopolitical methods developed through the social sciences: assessing public opinion, psychologically diagnosing large swaths of population (often along ethnic-linguistic and racial lines), and crafting propaganda in response to these social-scientific findings. In other words, governance was to operate as a never-ending, communicative feedback loop between public opinion and propaganda. The enforcement of communicative participation—and the information it yielded—would render barbed wire unnecessary once practices of information exchange were well established. "Participation" was therefore required of village detainees as a way of rehabilitating them, preparing them for integration within a soon-to-be capitalist, postcolonial state.[7]

A distinct concept of "democratic" participation thus becomes legible here, perhaps more legible still if one considers that, prior to staging "village" elections in the *kampung baru*, a similar procedure was enacted for gathering military intelligence. Routinely, detainees were queued up and required to anonymously deposit a slip of paper into a collection box.[8] The paper might be blank or might reveal information about other villagers' suspicious activities. Only after villagers had

6. On related uses of film as propaganda in the context of Nigeria, see Brian Larkin, *Signal and Noise: Media, Infrastructure, and Urban Culture in Nigeria* (Durham, N.C.: Duke University Press, 2008).

7. Tactics of Psy-Ops and the routines of villagization are described in Ghows, *The Malayan Emergency Revisited*.

8. Ghows, *The Malayan Emergency Revisited*.

thereby learned anonymous, participatory practices of po-
licing their co-villagers, only after a self-governing polity
emerged from processes of collective self-reporting, were villagers prepared to queue up for the ballot box. In voting, villagers also revealed their political tendencies to their British
administrators in an act of self-reporting. Democracy was established as a form of exchanging information, of replacing
the enclosures of barbed wire with the enclosures of feedback
loops between administrators and electorate. Participation
signaled one's willingness to enter into the circuit of information, as both consumer and provider.

During Kenya villagization, radio was the privileged
means of colonial transmission. The Kenya Broadcasting
Corporation was expanded in 1953 (in direct response to
the war against the KLFA) to include programming in nu-
merous local languages.[9] It was only in 1962, on the eve of
independence, that television broadcasting was established—
tellingly, not in the cities but in a small agricultural town
in the Rift Valley. In the research of Leonard Doob, whose
Communications in Africa McLuhan cites, electronic media
furnished means not only of disseminating Euro-American
messages among black Africans but also of gauging respon-
siveness to a widely circulated message.[10] Both television
and radio allow political views or consumer habits to be
measured and compared *en masse* before and after a rele-
vant transmission. Participation, in McLuhan's thinking, es-

9. Frederick K. Iraki, "Cross-media Ownership and the
Monopolizing of Public Spaces in Kenya" in *(Re)membering Kenya:
Identity, Culture, and Freedom,* ed. Mbũgua wa Mũngai and G. M. Gona
(Nairobi: Twaweza House, 2010), 142–59.

10. Leonard Doob, *Communications in Africa; A Search for
Boundaries* (New Haven, Conn.: Yale University Press, 1961).

sentially comprises an electronic version of pastoral power in which audiences commune voluntarily and actively with authority, rather than simply listening.[11]

11. On "pastoral power," see Michel Foucault, *Security, Territory, Population: Lectures at the Collège de France, 1977–78,* ed. Michel Senellart, trans. Graham Burchell (Basingstoke, UK; New York: Palgrave Macmillan and République Française, 2007); and Michel Foucault, "Omnes et Singulatim: Towards a Criticism of Political Reason," in *The Tanner Lectures on Human Values,* ed. Sterling McMurrin, 2:225–54 (Salt Lake City: University of Utah Press, 1981.)

6. Semiotic Poverty in the World

INSOFAR AS MCLUHAN'S "global village" seems to have been inspired by theories surrounding Kenya's detainment camps, we might invoke Giorgio Agamben's formulation of "the camp" as "the *nomos* of the modern." But the camp *qua* global village suggests a somewhat different *nomos* than the concentration camp, which Agamben cites as exemplary of biopolitical processes of reducing subjects to "bare life."[1] The concentration camp is not quite the right paradigm for describing the power latent in the concept of the global village, even despite certain similarities (both being, after all, "camps"). In the case of villagization, biopolitical sovereignty over life was not simply a matter of the right to extinguish life; it was governance over the psychic-social constitution of the individual subject.

By the mid-1950s, many colonial administrators began to view Kenya's independence as inevitable. The war became less about retaining colonial sovereignty than about safeguarding white settlers' property in the wake of decolonization and insuring that Kenya remained amenable to Britain's econom-

1. Giorgio Agamben, *Homo Sacer: Sovereign Power and Bare Life*, trans. Daniel Heller Roazen (Stanford, Calif.: Stanford University Press, 1998), 166–80.

ic and global military interests in the Cold War. Although Kenya's villagization has often been likened to the Holocaust camps, by the mid-1950s, British power of administering death in Kenya was increasingly superseded by apparatuses of soft power that sought to convert detainees not into *homo sacer*'s but into global villagers.

Unlike *homo sacer,* global villagers were to exercise the rights guaranteed by law but in a manner constrained—shrunken—by semiotic poverty. This form of semiotic disempowerment wouldn't necessarily be recognizable as *poverty,* given the semiotic amplitude that often engulfs the subject of nootechnologies. "Bare," then, isn't really the term to describe the electronically enchanted life of the global villager, even if the global villager is to be depoliticized, similar to the biopolitical subject of "bare life." The life of the global villager is to be captured by media, to be deeply, cognitively involved with that media, submerged in a rhythmic sensorium resembling the magical, arboreal semiosis Carothers described as innate to "the African mind." Through magical captivation by audiovisual media, a "state of exception" promulgated by violence is transformed into a nonexceptional state of popular participation.

Agamben has cited the phrase, "poverty in the world," used by Martin Heidegger to describe how animals receive and respond to sensory signals without, however, having access to "being."[2] Heidegger says that being can be disclosed only through human language, relative to which all other semiotic modes are impoverished.[3] Agamben does not explicitly draw any connection between "poverty in the world" and "bare life," but the former phrase might be used to connect Agamben's conception of bio-

2. Giorgio Agamben, *The Open: Man and Animal,* trans. Kevin Attell (Stanford, California: Stanford University Press, 2004), 49–56.

3. Agamben, *The Open,* 49–56.

politics with noopolitics. I use "semiotic poverty in the world" to describe a condition of relative impoverishment, a power imbalance. The global villager is grazed by word and image without possessing equal capabilities to leverage semiotic power toward political transformation. In other words, semiotic poverty is produced by a corollary semiotic affluence in the world—or *effluence*—which washes over us, precluding reply.

One virulent strain of semiotic poverty in the postcolonial world arose from the persistence of colonial languages as international lingua francas, a tendency that sheds light on another dimension of McLuhan's thinking. In the mid-1940s Ivor Armstrong Richards, a professor who deeply influenced McLuhan during the latter's doctoral studies at Cambridge University, devised Basic English and "English through Pictures" as a way to expand the international use of English, believing that a pared-down lexicon was requisite to transparent international communications and, consequently, world peace. Richards's insistence that a simplified English of merely 850 words would hone and clarify communication (rather than exacerbate the semiotic asymmetries of international power) anticipated McLuhan's concept of the global village, insofar as both models posited semiotic impoverishment as means of attaining perpetual peace. Conceived in the context of myriad anticolonial wars, the ideal of perpetual peace harbors violence within it, as suggested by the fact that colonial administrators in Malaya during the war against Malaya's Communist Party took a keen interest in Basic English.[4]

---

4. Tellingly, Richards's efforts to spread Basic English throughout China had captured the attention of Victor Purcell, working for the British Protectorate in Malaya on issues related to language and education. See Rodney Koeneke, *Empires of the Mind: I. A. Richards and Basic*

While Richards sought to eschew translation through a simplified lingua franca, McLuhan dreamt of computer technologies capable of circumventing language entirely so as to eradicate the differences between thought and language and the misunderstandings arising therefrom:

> Language as the technology of human extension, whose division and separation we know so well, may have been the "Tower of Babel" by which men sought to scale the highest heavens. Today computers hold out the promise of a means of instant translation of any code or language into any other code or language. The computer, in short, promises by technology a Pentecostal condition of universal understanding and unity. The next logical step would seem to be, *not to translate, but to by-pass languages in favor of a general cosmic consciousness* which might be very like the collective unconscious dreamt of by Bergson. The condition of "weightlessness," that biologists say promises a physical immortality, may be paralleled by *the condition of speechlessness that could confer a perpetuity of collective harmony and peace* [emphasis added].[5]

It is hard to imagine a greater semiotic poverty than what McLuhan envisions here—essentially a world dispossessed of language, save for computer code. Going a step beyond what Rosalind Morris has called "multilingualism against translation" (describing British language policies in Malaya), McLuhan dreams of a circum-lingualism against translation, which divests language of its semiotic powers and invests those powers within the work of audiovisual coding.[6]

English in China, 1929–1979 (Stanford, Calif.: Stanford University Press, 2004).

5. McLuhan, *Understanding Media*, 80.

6. "Multilingualism against translation" is how Rosalind Morris has described British policies of ethnic-linguistic segregation in Malaya, where the colonial production of ethno-linguistic roles and hierarchies depended on a strict control of literacy and language education along

However, the most peculiar dimension to McLuhan's Pentecostal fantasy is its proximity to his conception of the "tribal" world's aural semiosis, gleaned largely from Carothers. Carothers's thesis concerning the "African mind's" enthrall-ment to the authority of voice rested on the idea that written language revealed the arbitrary relation between signified and signifier, whereas spoken language produced an illusion of magical unity between words and the things they named. "Western man's" putative independence of thought was born of his supposed awareness of the fundamental difference and distance between signifier and signified, but it is precisely this distance between words and referents that McLuhan dreamed of eradicating through Pentecostal technologies.

Carothers's ideas concerning the illusory magic of spoken language likely drew from a much earlier book Richards had coauthored in 1927 with C. K. Ogden, *The Meaning of Meaning: A Study of the Influence of Language upon Thought and of the Science of Symbolism,* which had become stock reading for Anglophone scholars of semiotics and psychology. *The Meaning of Meaning* argued that language had long been linked to magic, insofar as words were believed to exercise a direct influence over their referents.[7] That McLuhan should have so rampantly cited Carothers's obscure article—published in a professional psychiatric journal—while never mentioning his own teacher's renowned work on a similar topic might be explained by a key difference in their respective arguments. Whereas Richards

---

ethnic lines. See Morris, "Imperial Pastoral: The Politics and Aesthetics of Translation in British Malaya," in *Representations,* Summer 2007, 159–94.

7. C. K. Ogden and I. A. Richards, *The Meaning of Meaning: A Study of the Influence of Language upon Thought and of the Science of Symbolism* (London: Kegan Paul, Trench, Trubner & Co., Ltd; New York: Harcourt Brace, 1927), 24–43.

and Ogden discussed how Western typographic propaganda had greatly expanded the deceptive magic of the written word, Carothers had, as we know, distinguished sharply between the rational habits of thought encouraged by literacy and the tendencies of magical thought promulgated through orality.

Additionally, Carothers's fixation on Africans' alleged orality appears to have drawn from the British wartime obsession with the loyalty oaths the KLFA administered to all fighters and to countless civilians. In this case it appears to have been the British who were dazzled by the magical power of the spoken word, as they went so far as to claim that the Kikuyu oaths had the power to utterly transform those who uttered them, so much as to alter the very color of their eyes and skin.[8] Following villagization, the oaths became the primary focus of British military strategists who were convinced that the war could be won only by countering the oaths' magical power. Even apart from the issue of propaganda then, the war was a semiotic war, insofar as what was at stake was how words operated socially and politically.

8. See Eileen Fletcher, "Hard Core of Mau Mau," TNA FCO 141/6604. See also the anonymous memorandum, "The Removal of Mau Mau Key Men from the Settled Areas," TNA FCO141/6608. Robert Blunt argues that British hysteria around the oath was largely used as propaganda in Great Britain and in the international community against widespread censure of Britain's war in Kenya. See Blunt, "Kenyatta's Lament: Oaths and the Transformation of Ritual Ideologies in Colonial Kenya," *The Journal of Ethnography* 3, no. 3 (2013), 167–93.

7. An Archaeology of De-oathing

ALL THIS is not to suggest that imposing semiotic poverty in Kenya was a simple matter, given that the KCA, along with many twentieth-century anticolonial and civil rights movements, had focused on education and literacy as a means of colonial resistance. The war, however, provided the opportunity for an excessive attack on the semiotic fabric of Kenyan society, ushering in practices of Christian pastoral power. In Europe, especially in the centuries prior to the expansion of literacy, semiotic poverty was deeply complicit with pastoral power, since the largely nonliterate Christian "flock" or laity had depended on the clergy to transpose God's text into spoken word. Michel Foucault, in his discussion of pastoral power says little about its semiotic dimensions, despite the fact that the rite of confession—which he briefly alludes to—must have been crucial in forging pastoral relations.[1] In this rite, the confessor's forbidden words and deeds are transposed to the pastor, thus bringing about an exchange of responsibility. To confess to the pastor one's former actions and words so as to be absolved of them is implicitly to exchange self-ownership and responsi-

1. On pastoral power, see Foucault, "Omnes et Singulatim," 225–54 See also Foucault, *Security, Territory, Population,* Lectures 5–9.

bility (what we could also call independence or self-rule) for pastoral solace and the magic of eschatological salvation. In thus divesting people of the consequences of their own words and actions, confession renders language into a medium of self-expropriation.

As it turns out, ritual confession was to constitute the central element of British efforts to win the war and rehabilitate village detainees, a policy based on the advice of Carothers and Louis Leakey, a paleo-anthropologist born in Kenya to missionary parents.[2] Nairobi's Municipal African Affairs Officer, Tom Askwith, heeding Carothers's and Leakey's beliefs in the potent effects of the KLFA loyalty oaths, recommended that the magic of the oaths be counteracted with what was effectively *another* magic: a ritual of de-oathing, which would involve confession and ritual purification, to be administered by Christian clerics, and which would constitute the decisive step toward the detainees' release from the camps.[3] Askwith had recently returned from a visit to Malaya where he'd observed Briggs' Plan of villagization. In conjunction with other colonial and military officers, he conceived of a more elaborate version of Malaya's *kampung baru's* for Kenya. "The Pipeline" would separate Kikuyu civilians and militants into several categories— on a gradation of black to white—based their level of loyalty or rehabilitation.[4] A person could progressively move toward

2. See "The Removal of Mau Mau Key Men from the Settled Areas," TNA FCO141/6608. See also Carothers, *The Psychology of Mau Mau*, 18–19, and Tom Askwith, *From Mau Mau to Harambee: Memoirs and Memoranda of Colonial Kenya*, ed. Joanna Lewis (Cambridge: Cambridge University Press, The African Studies Centre, 1995), 113–14.

3. Carothers, *Psychology of Mau Mau*, 18–19.

4. Askwith, *From Mau Mau to Harambee*, 113–16. On a history of the "Pipeline," see Caroline Elkins, *Imperial Reckoning: The Untold Story of Britain's Gulag in Kenya* (New York: Henry Holt, 2005), 107.

"white" after undergoing confession and de-oathing rituals.[5] Confessors' renunciations of the "Mau Mau" (i.e., KLFA) would be secretly tape recorded and then publicly broadcast at other detainment camps.[6]

In *The Sacrament of Language: An Archaeology of the Oath,* Agamben has highlighted the primordial performative role of oaths in endeavoring to stabilize the otherwise unstable relations between words and things.[7] At its origin, the oath offered some vestige of security—however weak—against that unstable relation through the voluntary election of language as socially binding (i.e., not magically binding, although the oath will also, he says, through its patent inability to truly bind words to things, open the way for both magic and violence). It is not necessarily that the oath was believed to *actually* bind words irrevocably to things; rather, it encouraged people to invest words with powers of social cohesion and personal responsibility.

Agamben points out that the oath is indeed a tacit acknowledgment of the impossibility of truly binding words to things and actions. (Indeed, if, as Carothers claimed, Africans had truly regarded words as magically bound to their referents, there would have been no need for oath-taking, no need to foreswear infidelity to one's words.) It could be said then that self-

---

5. Askiwth recommended Christian missionary activity as one of the methods of rehabilitating Kikuyu. Leakey's own parents were Christian missionaries in Kenya, and it seems likely that the mania for extracting confessions owes something to this Christian tradition. See Askwith, *From Mau Mau to Harambee,* 113.

6. "Kenya Plan for the Rehabilitation and Reabsorption of Mau Mau Detainees, Convicts, and Displaced Persons," September 27, 1955 from Secretary, Cabinet Office. TNA FCO 141/6263, 10.

7. Giorgio Agamben, *The Sacrament of Language: An Archaeology of the Oath,* trans. Adam Kotsko (Stanford, Calif.: Stanford University Press). see especially 4–8 and 22–23.

responsibility and self-rule—far from requiring, as Carothers argued, a dispassionate acceptance of the split between signified and signifier—are forged in the effort to interpolate one's self and choices within the murky space between signified and signifier, to operate consciously from within that instability, not to magically overleap it. Arguing that magico-religious practices and violence arise from the oath's inability to guarantee semiotic fidelity, Agamben opposes to the oath the invention of blasphemy: the uttering of words in vain, as signifiers without signifieds (for example, invoking the gods' names without intending to refer to the gods).[8] The effective power of such blasphemous speech lies not in signification but in magic and/or violence.

The British de-oathing campaign can be understood in similar terms, as reversing the impetus of the oath as speech act—its performance of semiotic and social fidelity—by compelling Kenyans to revoke the personal bond between self and semiosis, which is also a bond between self and society. The de-oathing campaign sought to deplete language of its performative power of self-assertion, carving out a different role for it—one of magical emanation. De-oathing, then, opened the way for "blasphemous" media to enter, media in which language functioned merely "in vain."

Take, for example, an anecdote McLuhan gleaned from Leonard Doob's sociological research on communications in Africa. Paraphrasing Doob, McLuhan described an "African who took great pains to listen each evening to the BBC news, even though he could understand nothing of it. Just to be in the presence of those sounds at 7 p.m. each day was important for him." McLuhan exaggerated Doob's account of the African's

8. Agamben, *The Sacrament of Language*, 40–43.

lack of comprehension to illustrate what was meant by "the medium is the message."[9] For the African listening to the BBC, what signified, according to McLuhan, was not language as such but simply the *presence* of sounds transmitted by electronic media. To be under the spell of the British broadcast without understanding a word of it was to be subject to a semiotic magic in which signifiers effectively had no signifieds. Media was, in some senses, already its own *Ur*-language.

If this recalls the Western tradition of logocentrism that Derrida would subsequently critique, it should be recalled that McLuhan's ideas also lean in the opposite direction from logocentrism, in that McLuhan believed that Europeans' derived their special cognitive independence from the detachment between the alphabetized word and its referent and the ensuing detachment between reader and author(ity).[10] This gives rise to the central aporia, noted earlier, in McLuhan's work: his simultaneous predilection for print media that detach signified from signifier and, on the other hand, for Pentecostal technologies capable of binding signified and signifier as a pure, *unmediating media*. (Clearly McLuhan—a devout Catholic—conceived of Pentecostal technologies in a magico-religious sense. As he later put it, "In Jesus Christ, there is no distance or separation between the medium and the message.") If there is an inverse relation between blasphemous media and Pentecostal communication, there is also, nonetheless, a chiasmus. Blasphemy describes the evacuation of the signified from the signifier, whereas Pentecostal technologies invert this operation, conserving the signified while obviating the need for signifiers. In either case, though, language becomes superfluous to itself, whether

9. McLuhan, *Understanding Media*, 20.
10. McLuhan, *Gutenberg Galaxy*, passim.

through its deliberate evacuation of sense or simply through its irrelevance. It is impoverished of its sociopolitical capacities, dissolved within a magic underwritten by the threat of violence.[11] The magical, aural semiosis Carothers described as the innate condition of "the African mind" was in fact what British sought to impose as the basis of postcolonial society: Replace the politics of oath-taking with the magical nonpolitics of aural incantation, and allow the nation to self-regulate according to noopolitical and agro-economic programs.

11. I draw from arguments Agamben elaborates throughout *The Sacrament of Language*.

8. Pastoral Beauty/Pastoral Power

THE COMPLICITY BETWEEN Britain's de-oathing campaign and its system of detainment attests to the importance of violence as means toward semiotic impoverishment, even as the British paved the way for softer forms of power. But soft power also seems to have played a role in persuading Kenyans to undertake the rituals of confession and de-oathing in the form of a massive program of land redistribution. Although detainees were not explicitly offered land as a direct incentive to confess, colonial administrators had clearly stipulated that KLFA members would be excluded from rights to land, and it was known that the colonial-loyalist chiefs who had been charged with the task of redistributing land were typically disposed to favor loyalists like themselves.[1] The program of land redistribution was, like confession, seen by the administration as a crucial component of rehabilitation, despite the fact that only some families would be granted land titles.

1. Kenneth Meadows, "Finding Jobs for the Out-of-Work Kikuyu," *East African Standard,* January 24, 1958. See also "Kenya Plan for the Rehabilitation and Reabsorption of Mau Mau Detainees, Convicts, and Displaced Persons, Sept. 27, 1955," TNA FCO141/6263.

Key to the five-year agricultural plan drafted by Swynnerton, as mentioned earlier, was the creation of a class of black cash-crop landowners to secure Kenya against the threat of further revolution. When Swynnerton was transferred from Tanganyika in 1949 to direct Kenya's agriculture department, his intent was to abolish obstacles preventing black Africans from cultivating tea and coffee, so as to enlarge the colony's tax base.[2] There were, however, major impediments to the transformations he envisioned: first, colonial settlers had long fought to protect their monopoly on tea and coffee plantations through quasi-legal means; second, native agricultural settlement patterns favored dispersed land holdings, which the administration deemed unsuitable to cash-crop agriculture; and finally there was the issue of procuring labor to execute the vast projects of land improvement required to expand arable land for cash-crop production. In 1952, the advent of war and villagization eliminated these obstacles: by convincing colonial settlers of the need to make certain concessions; by denuding the Rift Valley of people and agricultural production and thus enabling a sweeping scheme of land consolidation and redistribution; and finally by providing armies of poorly remunerated labor to execute major projects of dam irrigation, afforestation, and terracing.

In his five-year plan, Swynnerton outlined the amount of arable land to be alienated, the projected financial yields of particular crops, and infrastructural projects that would need to

2. Anne Thurston, *Smallholder Agriculture in Colonial Kenya: The Official Mind and the Swynnerton Plan* (Cambridge, UK: African Studies Centre, 1987), 8–12. See also John Lonsdale and Bruce Berman, "Coping with the Contradictions: The Development of the Colonial State in Kenya, 1895–1914," *Journal of African History* 20 (1979): 487–505.

be undertaken.[3] According to Swynnerton's calculations, the profits yielded by these changes should more than justify his request for a five-million-pound (later to become an almost eight-million-pound) development grant to Kenya.[4] The plots were to be farmed according to the administration's recommendations, which included planting methods, private enclosure of common pasturage, and terracing the land to minimize erosion. A large training corps assisted newly titled landowners in laying out their farms according to British norms.[5] The agricultural work projects were photographically documented by the colonial propaganda office, ushering in a resurgence of something resembling an eighteenth-century pastoral-Georgic aesthetic, depicting terraced fields and neatly enclosed pastures.[6] Drawing from such imagery, Elspeth Huxley's popular books disseminated photos of picturesque landscapes in the Rift Valley, replete with "before" and "after" shots, showing the region's transformation by Swynnerton's plan.[7] The images suggest a certain complicity between pastoral beauty and pastoral power.

According to Foucault, certain aspects of pastoral power were incorporated into methods of biopower; yet his lectures do not elaborate on the precise ways pastoral power is transformed or on how it might relate to movements he deemed

3. Swynnerton, *A Plan to Intensify the Development of African Agriculture.*

4. Thurston, *Smallholder Agriculture in Colonial Kenya,* 76.

5. Thurston, *Smallholder Agriculture in Colonial Kenya,* 114–17.

6. On the relation between the Georgic and pastoral, see Annabel Patterson, *Pastoral and Ideology: Virgil to Valéry* (Berkeley and Los Angeles: University of California Press, 1987), 133–92. See also Morris: "Imperial Pastoral."

7. See, for example, Elspeth Huxley, *On the Edge of the Rift: Memories of Kenya* (New York: Morrow, 1962).

crucial to the formation of biopolitics, such as the Physiocrats' concepts of *laissez-faire* or *laissez-passer*.[8] Implicitly there is a slippage between pastoral power and Physiocratic thought in the sense that governing humans (a pastoral construct) would depend on a thorough scientific knowledge of the *nature* of humans, since Physiocrats claimed to govern by allowing nature to function according to its own principles.

In the field of colonial power, however, the Physiocratic notion of governing according to nature is plunged into aporetic difficulties, which call for pastoral-aesthetic modes of resolution. The colonial construct of race raises the problem of different, irreconcilable versions of nature. Although the belief that different races possessed different natures provided a *raison d'être* of colonial governance, it also led to confusion concerning how to let a single *dominant* nature prevail amid other forms of nature that had to be upheld in order to be effectively governed (as can be seen with the urgent call to identify a properly "African medium").

In late colonial Kenya, the "nature" of Africans, as gleaned from anthropological and ethnopsychiatric analysis, was clearly at odds with what British construed as economic nature. British agricultural-economic theory (based on Physiocratic ideology) posited the need for land consolidation and titled ownership, which clearly controverted forms of land use and tenure considered integral—natural—to the social stability of Kenyans. Land consolidation, by rendering many landless, led inexorably to the ultimate deviation from African "nature". It led, that is, to urbanization. To transform anthropological nature in such a way as to render it amenable to economic nature—while appearing to not tamper with either one—was a

8. See Foucault's discussion of the eighteenth-century Physiocrats in *Security, Territory, Population*, 29–49.

complex process to be achieved largely through villagization, but the function of landscape aesthetics should also not be underestimated. Refurbishing eighteenth-century visual tropes, a neo-pastoralism helped render "natural" the violent transformations wrought by agricultural reform.

Art historians and literary scholars have often analyzed the ideological dimensions of eighteenth-century pastoral aesthetics and the related style of the picturesque, but without explicitly linking this ideology to Physiocratic doctrine.[9] A dominant scholarly account of the pastoral, articulated by Raymond Williams, ascribes the rise of the genre to a mounting sense of urban-industrial estrangement from nature and a subsequent nostalgia for rustic simplicity.[10] But it is not just any form of rusticity we encounter in pastoral scenes and poems. The binding motif of pastoral aesthetics—animal herding—can be read as emblematic of the principles of *laissez-faire* economics, which call for the unleashing of nature's own principles and processes.[11] The shepherd does not disrupt nature's processes but simply enforces the ambit within which the herd will conduct its own innate processes. In this sense the pastoral genre speaks eloquently to the transition Foucault describes from pastoral power to Physiocratic conceptions of governing by nature.

9. On the pastoral as ideology, see Patterson, *Pastoral and Ideology*.

10. On the idea of pastoralism as nostalgia for the rural or Golden Age (of which there are countless sources), see the following well-known texts: Raymond Williams, *The Country and the City* (Oxford: Oxford University Press, 1973); Leo Marx, *Machine in the Garden* (New York: Oxford University Press, 1964); Renato Poggioli, *The Oaten Flute: Essays on Pastoral Poetry and the Pastoral Ideal* (Cambridge, Mass.: Harvard University Press, 1975). Against the tendency to reduce the pastoral genre to a dialectic between city and country, see Paul Alpers, "What Is the Pastoral?" *Critical Inquiry* (Spring 1982): 437–60.

11. Foucault, *Security, Territory, Population*, 46–49.

For the theme of herding to appear so abundantly in European art, landscape, and literature at the moment of its economic demise attests, again, to more than simple nostalgia. Shepherding, although superseded by enclosure, becomes in pastoral imagery conceptually interchangeable with enclosure.[12] The enclosed pasture—far from disrupting the pastoralist ideal, as might be imagined—constitutes an even more perfect demonstration of *laissez-faire* rule, replacing human care (the inheritance of pastoral power) with a subtle technological intervention, a "program" within which animals can self-regulate. Instead of interfering in nature's processes, technologies of enclosure and related cartographies and bureaucratic procedures of land titling appear to support nature's processes, instantiating the ideal of indirect, techno-bureaucratic rule.

Enclosure, in eighteenth-century England and its colonies, was one of the basic strategies of "improving" land ("improve" being etymologically derived from "profit"), of returning the land to nature's intended state of productivity. The pastoral tropes of the eighteenth century underscored the connection between the *improvement of nature*—an expression that proliferates in European landscape and agricultural discourse at this time—and the conversion of land to private property.[13] For enclosure to appear as a more economical and natural form of shepherding, pastoralist paintings such as those by Jean-Antoine Watteau depict a fluidity between the landowning and herding classes, their shared gaiety serving as a form of ex-

12. Paul Alpers argues that pastoralism involves a metonymic substitution of the shepherd for society in general. Following his line of reasoning, it could be added that other such substitutions are at play, such as pastoral economies for new economic paradigms. See Alpers, *What Is Pastoralism?* (Chicago: University of Chicago Press, 1996).

13. See Vittoria DiPalma, *Wasteland: A History* (New Haven, Conn.: Yale University Press, 2014), chapter 2.

Figure 2. Photographer unknown. Land terracing as part of Swynnerton Plan, circa 1959. The National Archives INF 10/164.

change, emblematic of the actual transferal of land occurring through the enclosures movement. In pastoral paintings, this transferal is purged of historical conflict, appearing as a consensual circumstance, as the triumph of nature.

A photograph of Kenya collected by the colonial propaganda office on the eve of independence undertakes a similar sleight of hand, except that in this image the ruling class and the ruled do not commune directly with each other; they commune through the medium of the landscape. Two white men, with their backs turned to the camera, lean on a fence, gazing masterfully over a sweep of neatly terraced hills, while two black men pass behind them, also glancing at the hills but without pausing to drink it in. In an inversion of eighteenth-century pastoral paintings, this photograph suggests a transferal of land—from those who initially seized it to a new class of black landowners—that nonetheless conserves the power of the transferee, insofar as the colonist renders the organization of land and labor dependent on its own technique.

There is an economic corollary here to how participation in circuits of information was seen in Malaya as a noncoercive substitute for martial rule. As one journalist in Kenya explained, the most recalcitrant of KLFA supporters, being excluded from opportunities for landownership, could be removed to "land settlements sufficiently remote from contact with tribal or farming areas to allow *the substitution of an agricultural settlement in place of the barbed wire* and large numbers of armed guards which the detention system requires."[14] In the move toward more mediated forms of neocolonial influence, the nature of humans, agriculture, and global markets would be governed in concert through technological and bureaucratic interventions. The link between pastoral aesthetics and pastoral power lies in the capacity of the aesthetics to collapse the putative differences between anthropological and economic nature, enabling the former to be intimately governed according to the laws of the latter. This is brought about through images that elide contradictions and conflicts and, on the other hand, through technological programs—semiotic, spatial, and agricultural—that subsume anthropological nature within the prerogatives of the economic.

14. "Problem of Resettling Dangerous Men," *East African Standard*, August 4, 1955, TNA FCO 141/6324.

9. Owning Land/Owning Letters

NEO-PASTORALIST IMAGERY of Kenya's agricultural trans-formation constitutes an aesthetic semiosis of sorts, but the landscape is simultaneously encoded through nonsemiotic means, through a calculus of risk absorption. Swynnerton justified his application for development funds in terms of both its politically stabilizing effects and its economic output, outlining the precise crop yields and revenues to result from this investment.[1] If previously Kenyans had managed risk in part through semiotic performance and ritual (through oath-taking, for example, as argued by Robert Blunt), an agrarian capitalist regime of risk calculation was to be backed by land as guarantor.[2] Semiotic pledges of responsibility were displaced by another form of presumed fidelity: fidelity to the soil through proper stewardship of its productive nature, a task requiring private ownership and enlightened agricultural methods as its basis.

1. Swynnerton, *A Plan to Intensify the Development*.
2. Robert Blunt, "Kenyatta's Lament: Oaths and the Transformation of Ritual Ideologies in Colonial Kenya," *The Journal of Ethnography* 3, no. 3 (2013): https://www.haujournal.org/index.php/hau/article/view/hau3.3.008.

Soil has long served as collateral against the speculation of capital, tethering the latter's vicissitudes back to a reassuringly solid anchor. Perhaps for this reason, *inter alia,* land was crucial to the European discourse of nationality that emerged concomitantly with the rise of capitalism. According to the eighteenth-century Physiocrat François Quesnay and his disciple, Anne Robert Jacques Turgot, landownership as a form of political rule was the only way to guarantee a politics invested in the general interest of the nation.[3] Political power had long been derived from control of land and labor, but this relationship received a distinct articulation in Physiocratic doctrine in three respects: first, in Turgot's recommendation for a "juste distribution des voix," which would apportion votes according to a landlord's yearly rent; second, in Turgot's claim that, through this national voting structure, the monarch would be excused from directly legislating on all matters, allowing him to instead "govern like God, according to general laws"; and third (anticipating Carothers), by designating "the village" as the basic unit of national governance, whose interests would be represented by landlords.[4] In other words, the divine right of kings could be supplanted by a system of natural of law linked to the ownership of soil.

---

3. Turgot reasoned that by the fact of owning land, landowners were invested in the economic and social welfare of the nation, such that they could be expected to justly support taxation and large public-works projects to the general benefit of the nation. See Anne Robert Jacques Turgot, "Mémoire sur les municipalités a ètablir en France," in *Oeuvres Posthumes de M. Turgot* (Lausanne: 1787): 22–27.

4. Turgot writes: "[V]ous pourriez gouverner comme Dieu par des loix génerales, si les parties intégrantes de votre empire, avoient une organisation régulière." Turgot, "Mémoire sur les municipalités," 6. On the establishment of voting structure, see Turgot, "Mémoire sur les municipalités," 16–35.

Although presaging the demise of divine monarchial right, this conception of parliamentary legislation still conserved the magico-religious element of divine right. Turgot offered little explanation of why votes should be premised on land ownership, beyond an unsubstantiated assumption that to own land was to be deeply invested in the welfare of the nation and its people.[5] It appears, within the context of Physiocratic thought, that the natural laws operative in the terrestrial world are magically transposed from land to landlord, conferring to the latter the right and responsibility to govern the earth and its human and nonhuman processes. The landlord's ability to ventriloquize the natural law of the land presupposes an affluence of *voix* (designating both "vote" and "voice") as an instrument of power.

As noted, Physiocratic doctrine was far from unique in linking sovereignty to the management of land. Among countless such examples, it has been widely noted that for nineteenth- and early twentieth-century Kikuyu society, acquiring land was a constituent part of males' passage into adulthood, enabling them to marry and assume the responsibilities of a patriarch. The land shortages caused by settler colonialism did not only materially impoverish many Kikuyu, they also created an epidemic of prolonged adolescence for young men deprived of the responsibilities of adulthood. It is likely that the KCA literacy campaign had an important function in this respect, as literacy provided a different path to adulthood, as it redirected a crucial instrument of colonialism toward purposes of decolonization.

It should be recalled that at various points in the history of Euro-America's first national republics, landownership and

---

5. Turgot writes: "[L]es propriétaires du sol . . . sont liés à la terre par leur propriété ; ils ne peuvent cesser de prendre intérêt au canton où elle est placée." Turgot, "Mémoire sur les municipalités," 24.

literacy numbered among the basic qualifications for political suffrage. The very term "suffrage," formerly referring to intercessory prayers, was strongly suggestive of pastoral power, indicating the right to speak on behalf of others, essentially so as to save them from themselves. While it made sense in some respects for a republic of letters to premise political rights on a person's ability to parse newspapers, pamphlets, and books, the additional stipulation of landownership argues for a different interpretation of the linking of suffrage and literacy.[6] Just as Physiocrats' mystification of nature made landownership into a form of imperial subjectivity enabling landlords to speak for others, so literacy requirements bespoke a privileged form of semiotic subjectivity enabling the literate to ventriloquize the *nature* inhering to the nonlettered, anthropological remainder of humanity. The landless are relegated to muteness because they are landless, and they are condemned to landlessness because they are deemed mute: lacking, that is, the semiotic self-consciousness required of political thought.

6. One needs only turn to *Letters from an American Farmer,* written amid the United States' war for independence, to see the inherent connection drawn at the time between land ownership, literacy, and self-governance. See J. Hector St. John de Crèvecoeur, *Letters from an American Farmer,* ed. Susan Manning (Oxford: Oxford University Press, 1997).

10. Terra-Power

AN EIGHTEENTH-CENTURY NOTION that literacy constituted a form of politically enfranchised, self-ruling subjectivity resurfaces in the mid-twentieth century not only in the work of Carothers and McLuhan, or in the spurious literacy tests used to bar black Americans from voting, but also in the agricultural policies the British and the World Bank imposed on Kenya in its transition to independence. To resolve the political problem posed by white settlers' demands for remuneration for property (should they choose to flee independent Kenya), the British devised the Million-Acre-Settlement Scheme, to be sponsored jointly by Britain and the World Bank. The scheme allowed Kenyans to purchase land from white settlers (at overvalued rates set by the British) with the help of bank loans. Subject to the World Bank's criteria, the scheme promulgated ownership of medium-large plantations, despite political pressures from many Kenyans to accommodate smallholders and collectives.[1] The historian Christopher Leo has shown how the Bank privileged "progressive farmers," generally meaning that

---

1. Christopher Leo, "The Failure of the 'Progressive Farmer' in Kenya's Million-Acre Settlement Scheme," *The Journal of Modern African Studies* 6, no. 4 (December 1978): 619–38.

they selected loan recipients from among a literate bourgeoisie (who often had other forms of urban professional employment), not from among the pool of people who most urgently needed land.[2]

According to World Bank criteria, poor nonliterate farmers could not be depended on to repay loans. Yet the results of the Million-Acre scheme suggested otherwise. Leo has pointed out that, contrary to the claims made by agricultural experts at the time, Kenya's smallholdings turned out to be more productive per hectare than large plantations, even despite the fact that smallholders were granted the least arable lands.[3] Leo's research only reaffirms what colonial agricultural experts had already observed in the 1930s and '40s—that black Kenyans' small farms were generally more economically viable than whites', despite the advantages enjoyed by the latter.[4] Given this evidence, the privileges accorded to progressive farming seem to constitute little more than the assertion of a class-based system of power, upheld by the tenet that a certain cognitive disposition (that of a literate bourgeoisie) was needed to properly govern the nature of land.

In the first pages of this essay, I stated that noopolitics ideally should be analyzed in their entanglement with other strains of power. Of particular interest in the case of Kenya is a category of power that has gone unnamed in the annals of scholarship, although aspects of it certainly appear in Marx and in Marxian scholarship, in the environmental humanities,

2. Leo, "The Failure of the 'Progressive Farmer'"

3. Leo, "The Failure of the 'Progressive Farmer.'"

4. John Lonsdale, "The Depression and the Second World War in the Transformation of Kenya," in *Africa and the Second World War*, ed. David Killingray and Richard Rathbone (New York: St. Martin's Press, 1986), 97–142.

and (rather latently) in Foucault's discussion of biopower. This category, which I call terra-power, refers to the harnessing of the earth's bioproductive capacities, involving techniques of labor management, techniques of destruction and infrastructural construction, and techniques of cultivation, all tending toward the physical reorganization of the earth's humans and nonhumans. Appearing in antiquity with the rise of large-scale agriculture and a corresponding division of labor, terra-power is the foundation of what Ulrich Beck calls "risk society," reminding us that the latter is not in fact a twentieth-century phenomenon but is implicated in the very advent of agricultural production, which has always been a technology for mitigating risk while, in the process, constantly producing new risks.[5] Or rather, terra-power is a technology for *redistributing* risk over time and across different strata of society. Involved in both risk production and risk absorption, terra-power has been long linked to class struggle, which, at its historical base, concerns how the burden of agricultural risks, the burdens of labor, and the boon of agricultural surpluses should be distributed among the classes.

The late nineteenth-century development of agricultural futures trading transposed this distribution of risk into a self-regulating system. Going a step further, digital cell-phone technologies are now touted as a means of putting Third World farmers directly in touch with agricultural futures markets.[6] Nootechnologies thus support terra-power, attempting to de-

5. Ulrich Beck, *Risk Society: Towards a New Modernity,* trans. Mark Ritter (London: Sage Publications, 1992).

6. See, for example, Tapash Talukdar, "Farmers Too See a Bright Futures in Trade," *The Economic Times,* January 16, 2011: http://economictimes.indiatimes.com/money-you/farmers-too-see-a-bright -futures-in-trade/articleshow/7294874.cms.

fuse class struggle by converting every Third World farmer into a petty risk-bearing capitalist. These digital tools clearly serve as instruments of what Stiegler calls collective individuation, but it should be remembered that collective individuation is also conducted through architecture and that the global village is an architectural configuration, one facilitating noopolitics through the distribution of people so as to direct them toward particular semiotic forms of subjectivity.[7] Supporting processes of nootechnical individuation are the architectures that organize collective modes of existence and collective identities.

7. Stiegler is drawing his idea of individuation from the work of Gilbert Simondon. See especially Stiegler, *Decadence of Industrial Democracies (Mécréance et Descrédit, tome 1: La decadence des dömocraties industrielles)*, trans. Daniel Ross and Susan Arnold (Cambridge, UK: Polity, 2011).

11. Monuments, Villages, Camps

KENYA'S VILLAGIZATION wove together noopolitics, biopower, and terra-power through the military deployment of a simple spatial device—villagization—which worked in concert with communications technologies, the reorganization of labor, and massive programs of land consolidation and redistribution. So as to buffer against political unrest prompted by land shortages, villagization would provide an alternate form of social organization and habitation. By conglomerating detainees in quasi-urban forms of density and thus facilitating access to traveling cinema and radio vans, villagization would endeavor to convert agents of discourse into subjects of media reception. By orienting village schools toward vocational and agricultural training more than toward rhetorical competency, villagization would attempt to instate semiotic poverty amidst economic modernization.[1] By relocating former city dwellers into villages, large-scale political organization might be inhibited. By replacing people's livelihoods with conscripted labor compensated with forms of welfare, detainees would be rendered economically dependent.

1. "Report on Future of the Athi River Detention Camp, September 1954," TNA FCO 141/5688. See also TNA FCO 141/6492.

As a means of producing new forms of dependency on the brink of Kenya's independence, villagization might be considered as an obverse to a very different architecture appearing a decade after Kenya's independence, a postcolonial monument that attests to the dialectical complexities of modernization and postcoloniality. In the wake of independence, Kenya's dominant political party, the Kenya African National Union (KANU), elected to build its new headquarters in Nairobi on a plot immediately adjacent to the national parliament. Responding to legal objections against funding such facilities with federal resources, President Kenyatta appended to the party headquarters a public convention center with a hotel tower, and the building was rebranded as the Kenyatta International Convention Centre (KICC). As the building was to be completed in time to host the 1973 conference of the World Bank, it was outfitted with sophisticated Simultaneous Interpretation Equipment, similar to what had been installed at the United Nations Headquarters in New York.[2]

The building quickly became the foremost architectural emblem of Kenya's postcolonial modernization. It was approached through a procession of terraces, abounding with vegetation, ramps, and fountains. If Swynnerton's Plan had been a garden, it would look like this: the recent taming of water, agriculture, and slopes symbolized respectively in the building's surrounding water features, its lush greenery, and its terraced plinths and gently graded ramps. The interior of the KICC amphitheater conformed to what was by the mid-1960s a fairly standard global type. Ringed by concentric, elevated seating sections, the room was lit from above by skylights that cast an ecclesiastical light, and it was crowned by the representation of a terrestrial

2. "Architecture and Planning in Kenya," in *Arquitectura Madrid*, 1966: 2–46.

globe suspended above the speaker's dais. Over the years, the building became a venue mostly for industry meetings and international conferences on economic development. As a monument to the nation's power, it attested to the links between voice (dramatized through the impressive amphitheater), the global market (the hotel tower dominating Nairobi's skyline), and the agrarian base of capital (the building's gardens). The building emblemized Kenya's coming of age as a nation-state, and yet the nation's "maturity" or "development"—dependent as it was on the power of agrarian capital—contained within it the husk of that other architectural type, villagization, which had been designed to produce a perpetual state of semiotic and political immaturity.

The costly monumentality of the KICC represented the concentration of party-based power brought about (in part) by villagization and the Swynnerton Plan, with their vastly inequitable distribution of landed property. KANU was largely an affiliation of Kenya's two most urbanized ethnic-linguistic groups, the Luo and the Kikuyu. While Kenyans certainly defied Carothers's fantasy of an innately nonliterate "African mind," the nation's quick mastery of media technologies (begun decades earlier in its anticolonial struggle) exacerbated in some ways the differences between an educated elite and the rest of society (although, relative to many nations, Kenya boasted high literacy rates).[3] Related to issues of landownership, KANU's grip on national politics was bolstered by frequent handouts of land to curry support.[4] Questions of land governance came to

3. See Frederick K. Iraki, "Cross-media Ownership and the Monopolizing of Public Spaces in Kenya," in *(Re)membering Kenya: Identity, Culture, and Freedom,* ed. Mbũgua wa Mũngai and G. M. Gona (Nairobi: Twaweza House, 2010), 142–59.

4. Several years ago the Ngundu Report was made public, revealing

63

a head in the early years of independence when the federal government waged its own violent villagization campaign against the semi-nomadic ethnic Somalis living in Kenya's Northern Frontier District.

As such, it would be naïve to see the KICC only as a heroic concretization of postcolonial independence. Like many nationalist monuments, it worked through an ambiguous chain of associations, metonymic substitutions, and seductions, masking the fact that sovereignty lies not with agrarianism in general but with the state's perpetual conversion of land to capital and vice-versa. And the building's Simultaneous Interpretation Equipment (a kind of "multi-lingualism against translation"), in simulating a Pentecostal condition, obfuscated the actual semiotic rifts demarcating the global village from the capital city. The monumentality of the KICC assisted in this work of obfuscation because architecture is only ever partly semiotic, and thus can elide the semiotic rifts cutting through society. Approaching McLuhan's dream of Pentecostal technologies, architecture signifies by what it *is*—by the reality that it produces—not through signifiers as such.

rampant political corruption related to land trade. See Catherine Boone, "Land Conflict and Distributive Politics in Kenya," *African Studies Review* 55, no. 1 (2012): 75–103; http://www.jstor.org/stable/41804129.

12. "The Nomos of the Modern"

WE ARE ALL IN VARIOUS WAYS global villagers—semiotically impoverished relative to the nootechnologies that form our cultural and cognitive habitus. The specific history of Kenya's transition to independence is intended to exemplify a more global tendency according to which responsibility (or what Stiegler has also called "maturity") is deferred through the instatement of semiotic magic as a substitute for self-rule.[1] Returning to Agamben's thesis that the Holocaust camp constitutes the "nomos of the modern," I would propose that the methods of power most paradigmatic of the present were not those.[2] based on explicit systems of exclusion, but rather the ways that exclusionary practices were interwoven with means of liminal inclusion and interpenetration allowing hierarchical categories such as class and race to remain intact but never too rigidly When exploitation—rather than expulsion—of difference reigns, then power need not distinguish strictly and irrevocably between which groups are internal and external to the polis. The categories allow for interpenetration and ambiguity even while they are maintained.

1. Stiegler, *Taking Care of Youth and the Generations.*
2. Agamben, *Homo Sacer,* 166–80.

The "nomos of the modern" is not directed primarily toward irrevocable exclusions, as accomplished through genocide or *de jure* political and spatial apartheid. The paradigmatic camp might be described more as a "village," a global village that operates as a device of conversion, filtration, and connectivity: shaping, sifting, and weaving together different modes of subjectivity, distributing them along broad, fluid continuums suitable to the ownership and nonownership of land, capital, and letters. The paradigmatic camp is to be found less in the early and most brutal phases of Kenya villagization than in its strategies of rehabilitation, in the "Pipeline" system of progressively (and magically) converting people from the status of detainees into a subtle gradation of other class- and ethnic-based statuses.

What this means is that the global villagers can belong fully to an independent nation, while being nonetheless unable to effectively leverage the rights of citizenship, rights that depend on semiotic affluence. Between the poles of citizenship and noncitizenship are the various gradations of quasi-citizenship through which sovereignty can *legitimately* operate (i.e., minimizing its states of exception). Biopolitics might be differently understood if we added to the problem of "bare life" the fact that depoliticization often comes garbed in the lineaments of normal, participatory forms of inclusion, which bear little kinship to the logic of death camps. This depoliticized life is often perfectly coterminous with sensual pleasures, with material nourishment, and with social-political involvement in an (impoverished) public sphere. And if we were to complicate the model of "bare life" by considering the effects of noopolitics (and their entanglement with terra-power), perhaps the complex figure crystallizing at this nexus of power—the figure of the global village—would suggest somewhat different strategies of resistance.

13. We, the Global Villagers

IN ITS BROADEST SENSE, the "global village" designates a fairly ubiquitous condition of semiotic disempowerment in the face of mass media. Yet more specifically and owing to the unique ability of electronic mass-media to operate across distances and in the absence of systems of public education, the global village names a paradigm for instating semiotic poverty as means of facilitating the conversion of agrarian land into agrarian capital (as is now transpiring apace in Africa and Latin America). A battle against the perpetual conversion of land into capital and vice-versa (a battle often waged in the name of environmental justice or indigenous rights) must therefore be conceived also as a "battle for intelligence," to use Stiegler's expression.[1] Semiotic poverty[2]—whether belonging to the nonliterate or to those whose limited rhetorical training fails to guard against what Talal Assad has called "seductive speech"—such poverty is tantamount to what being "landless" has meant in other times and places: to be without means of economic and polit-

---

1. Stiegler is interpreting Kant's idea of intellectual but also historical maturity and the "battle" this requires. Stiegler, *Taking Care of Youth and the Generations,* chapter 2.

2. McLuhan, *Gutenberg Galaxy,* 21.

ical independence.[3] Wherever terra-power and noopolitics collaborate, shuttling between agrarian society and the global market, is where the villagers of the global village can be found.

Such a battle for intelligence is always already being fought. Every class conflict, every anticolonial war, and every civil rights movement is to some extent a battle for intelligence, a battle for rights to education, to semiotic empowerment, to the means of rendering one's stories public, and to the political capabilities deriving therefrom. Keeping this in mind, a battle for intelligence must not be approached as if noopolitics (or, for that matter, capital) operated homogenously across the globe. Semiotic technologies are differently leveraged and accessed in global North versus South, in differently educated classes, and in cities versus villages. We are all semiotically impoverished to varying degrees, according to accidents of birth and the educational privileges subsequently withheld or conferred. A battle for intelligence would have to acknowledge these differences (these accidents of birth and all the power differentials deriving therefrom). Colonialisms and the techno-humanitarian movements that are often heir to colonial logics have long employed techno-aesthetic magic as means of elision—as means of obfuscating the societal differences they help produce. In a direct inversion of this method, a battle for intelligence would have to constantly acknowledge those differences as the preliminary basis for overcoming them.

3. Talal Assad, "Free Speech, Blasphemy, and Secular Criticism," in *Is Critique Secular? Blasphemy, Injury, and Free Speech* (New York: Fordham University Press, 2013), 25–26.

Acknowledgments

I express thanks to Columbia University's Institute of Comparative Literature and Society. During my fellowship there in 2015 I wrote the original draft for this essay.

Ginger Nolan is a postdoctoral fellow in urban studies at Basel University.